HOOD COUNTY PUBLIC LIBRARY

105178

AF443711

superstars!
superstars!
superstars!
CREATIVE EDUCATION SPORTS SUPERSTARS

rosi mittermaier
rosi mittermaier

rosi mittermaier

by Jay H. Smith

illustrated by
John Keely

CREATIVE EDUCATION
CHILDRENS PRESS

Published by Creative Educational Society, Inc., 123 South Broad Street, Mankato, Minnesota 56001. Copyright © 1977 by Creative Educational Society, Inc. International copyrights reserved in all countries. No part of this book may be reproduced in any form without written permission from the publisher. Printed in the United States.

Library of Congress Cataloging in Publication Data

Smith, Jay H.
  Rosi Mittermaier.
  SUMMARY: A biography of the German skier whose performance in the 1976 Olympics and World Cup competition have won her worldwide acclaim.
  1. Mittermaier, Rosi, 1950- —Juvenile literature.
  2. Skiers—Germany, West—Biography—Juvenile literature.
  [1. Mittermaier, Rosi, 1950- 2. Skiers] I. Title.
GV854.2.M57S63   796.9'3'0924 [B] [92]   76-39923
ISBN 0-87191-544-8

rosi
maier
termaier
mitter
rosi
mittermaier
ermittermaier

The moon raced across the sky. Down below, nestled among the Alps, lay the sleeping village of Reit im Winkl.

The night was very still in this remote corner of the West German province of Bavaria. The only sound to be heard was the song of the wind.

The dark peaks of the Zahmer Kaiser mountains stood facing the village. Further to the left towered the glacial cliffs of the Wilder Kaisers, shimmering like pale blue gemstones in the moonlight.

It was shortly before dawn. Soon the summits of the Kaisers would take on the reddish hue that mountain people call alpenglow.

Already, the silent village was beginning to wake. Before the sun had climbed very high, Reit im Winkl would be humming with activity.

It was cold that February morning in 1976. But the sun was bright and there was hardly any wind. The townspeople were pleased with the weather the day had brought them. It was perfect for the celebration they were planning. Today they would welcome Rosi Mittermaier home in triumph.

At the Winter Olympic Games in Innsbruck, Austria, Rosi had astonished the world with a brilliant display of Alpine skiing. She raced off with three medals: two gold and one silver. She won the first two events, the downhill and the slalom, easily. And then she finished second in the giant slalom — missing a third gold medal by a fraction of a second.

When she was done, Rosi had given the greatest overall Alpine performance in Olympic history.

Rosi's achievement thrilled the people of Reit im Winkl and made them proud. But perhaps more than anything else, they were glad for Rosi herself.

Many of them had known her all her life. They had watched Rosi grow and change as she reached each new step of maturity. And always they had found her delightful. Long before she ever skied her first race, Rosi had brought joy to the village . . . .

She was only two years old when she put on skis for the first time. Before long, Rosi wanted to ski down to Reit im Winkl from her house in the suburb of Winklmoosalm higher up the mountain.

Soon she was expert enough to do exactly that. Then to the delight of the townspeople, young Rosi would come darting down the mountainside like an Alpine bird. Her laughter rang across the snow as she entered the village.

It was still quite early on the morning of Rosi's homecoming. But already Reit im Winkl had a festive look. Colorful banners were flying everywhere. And the newly-polished bells atop the old Bavarian farmhouses gleamed in the sunlight.

From the village kitchens came the wonderful smells of chickens roasting and fancy pastries baking. The cooks hurried about, preparing other foods for the banquet that evening.

There would be mounds of salt rolls called *salztangen* and sausages smothered in mustard and radishes as large as turnips.

Hundreds of fish would be roasted on sticks over charcoal fires. And these *steckelfisch* and all the other strange and delicious things would be washed down with barrels and barrels of dark German beer.

As they went about their work, the villagers thought of the bright-eyed child Rosi once was and of the charming young woman she had become.

On her adventures down the mountain from Winklmoosalm so long ago, Rosi had made skiing look like the easiest thing in the world. And at Innsbruck, she had made it look even easier.

The townspeople also thought of the years in between. Things had not gone so easily for Rosi then.

Rosi's success had come late in her career. She had been on the world ski scene so long that many of the other skiers affectionately called her ''Granny'' and ''Mama''.

Of all the women who competed in the Alpine events at the Innsbruck Olympics, Rosi was the oldest. At 25, an age when most female skiers have long since retired from major competition, Rosi had suddenly hit her peak.

Rosi began her long climb to the top in 1967. Only 16, she left her native village to join the West German team on a new ski tour called the World Cup of Alpine Skiing.

The World Cup had just been organized. Instantly, the racers were enthusiastic about it. They especially liked its point-scoring system—a new concept in skiing.

In the past, the world's top Alpine skiers were rated on the basis of one or two headline-winning races. But under the World Cup point system, they would be ranked according to the results of many races over a whole season.

Since then, the World Cup has come to rival the

Olympics in importance, if not in glamor. Now many people who know skiing well feel that the World Cup provides the ultimate test of skiing superiority.

Rosi had a good time on the 1967 tour. It was exciting to visit cities she had never seen before. But most of all, she loved the racing.

Rosi's enthusiasm, however, was not enough to make up for her lack of experience. She did not win a single race or finish very high in the World Cup standings. But when the tour was over that season, she was a better skier than she had been when it began.

Rosi felt more sure of herself when she returned to the World Cup tour in 1968. As a result, she continued to improve.

But at the Olympics that year in Grenoble, France, Rosi's confidence deserted her. Plagued by nervousness, she performed poorly in all three events.

In 1969 Rosi won her first World Cup race—the slalom at Schruns, Austria. But more important than that, she skiied with greater consistency all season long.

Every season from 1970 to 1974, Rosi continued to advance in the standings. She won some races, but fewer than she might have. Often when victory was in

her grasp, Rosi would make a small technical error or lose her concentration for a moment. And the race would be lost.

Rosi went to the Olympics for the second time in 1972. She hoped to do better in Sapporo, Japan, than she had done in Grenoble. And at first she did, coming in a strong sixth in the downhill. But then her Olympic jitters returned, and Rosi was never in contention in the slalom and giant slalom.

By 1975, Rosi had established herself as one of the best technical skiers in the world. And her confidence seemed to grow with every race. Late in the season she was in second place in the overall World Cup standings, closing in on the leader, Annemarie Moser-Proell of Austria.

But then in Innsbruck, on the same slope where one year later she would race to Olympic glory, Rosi was knocked down by a skiing tourist. Her arm broken, Rosi had to give up her hopes of beating Moser-Proell.

When Rosi was six months old, a goat jumped into her baby carriage and nearly suffocated her. At two, she ate some rat poison and almost died. And the list goes on and on.

Rosi took her latest bit of bad luck in stride. Things like

that were always happening to her. Throughout her skiing career there had been many failures and falls. But Rosi feels that the good fortune she has had outweighs the bad.

"I have been born under a lucky star," she once said.

That star was shining brightly when Rosi began the 1976 World Cup tour. Immediately she opened up big leads in both the overall and the slalom championships.

And she had increased these leads by early February. Then there was a break in the tour so that skiers could go to Innsbruck to compete in the 1976 Winter Olympics.

Rosi felt remarkably calm in Innsbruck. She was free at last of the inner turmoil which had troubled her at the Olympics before.

There was hardly any pressure on Rosi from the outside, either. Although she ranked in the top ten in the world in all three Alpine events, Rosi was not expected to win any of them.

The experts predicted that Rosi would get only one medal—a bronze in the slalom. Because of her commanding lead in World Cup slalom competition,

Rosi should have been the favorite in this event at
Innsbruck. But the experts believed that once again
Rosi would not be able to handle Olympic pressure.

Rosi didn't completely agree. She was confident of
finishing higher than third in the slalom. And she
thought she might have an outside chance for the
bronze medal in the giant slalom. But as far as the
downhill was concerned, Rosi had to admit her
chances were remote.

Rosi had never won a major downhill race before.
And she was much too realistic to hope for a miracle
at Innsbruck. She knew she had the technical ability to
handle the course, but lacked the blazing speed the
race requires.

There were so many fast downhillers at Innsbruck. The
favorite was Marie-Therese Nadig of Switzerland, who
had won the gold medal at Sapporo in 1972.

Suddenly Nadig was knocked out of competition by
influenza. Even then, Rosi didn't think she had a
chance. The new favorites were Brigitte Totschnig of
Austria and Cindy Nelson of the United States. And if
they faltered, there were still others to take their place.

Rosi began preparing for the downhill. At first she

made slow, deliberate turns simply to get used to the feel of the course. With every run she became more used to its bumps and twisting turns. On the day of the race, she would be hurtling down the mountain at 60 miles per hour. She couldn't afford to be surprised by anything it had to offer. Any rough spot she hadn't learned to handle could throw her off balance. Then she would either lose precious time or fall.

Most of the other skiers were complaining about the treacherous course. But not Rosi. The icier the course, the more important her technical skill and control became. Rosi knew the other racers would become cautious now and that would slow them down a bit. She hoped the course would stay the way it was.

Tensions were mounting among the other skiers. Cindy Nelson completed only four of her nine practice runs, falling and missing gates and crying in despair. Brigitte Totschnig and the other Austrian skiers were feeling pressure to perform well in front of the home crowd.

With each practice run she made, Rosi grew more confident. She felt she was beginning to master the mountain. She had found its ''fall line''—the shortest way down. On the day of the race, Rosi thought she might possibly take a bronze medal in the downhill— if she skied her very best.

Just before the race, Rosi's coach Klaus Mayr was

standing at the starting line with her, giving advice. But Rosi wasn't listening. Racers never do, at this time. She smiled, alone with her thoughts.

Rosi shot out of the starting gate like a bullet. Attacking the course fiercely, she had absolutely no thought of its danger. She crouched low over her skis, her poles tucked under her arms. She was careful not to become airborne, for that would lose time. So she kept her skis flat to the icy snow. She looked far ahead to see what lay beyond, and her reflexes took care of what was at hand.

It was a beautiful, daring run. And it was also the best. Rosi won the gold medal with a time of one minute 46.16 seconds. Later she said, ''I had not the courage to look at the timing. I looked at the faces and I knew what had happened.''

Brigitte Totschnig had to be content with the silver medal. And Cindy Nelson, her composure regained, took the bronze.

Everyone was amazed by what Rosi had done. And she herself was wide-eyed with wonder. She couldn't stop giggling. ''I can't believe that it's me who has won,'' she exclaimed.

Millions of TV viewers around the world were immediately captivated by Rosi. She had raced brilliantly. And she was as refreshing as mountain air.

CERP
8

Suddenly Rosi was a bright new celebrity everywhere. And in West Germany she was a national heroine, the first from her country to win a gold medal in Alpine skiing since 1960.

Rosi spent the next three days quietly, preparing her mind for the slalom. Above all, she wanted to retain her concentration.

The slalom course was set up by officials just two hours before the race. They placed poles with green and red flags in various patterns along the course. In some places there was only one pole. In others, there were two poles side by side. These are called gates because they form a kind of doorway. There were many patterns to test the technical skill of the skiers. There were hairpin turns and four-gate flushes, which are four gates lined up close together.

No practice was allowed for the slalom. The skiers had to look at the mountain and memorize the course, without actually getting close to it. Rosi studied the course and ran it in her mind several times.

The skiers would race the course twice. The gold medal would go to the one with the best combined time. Rosi planned her strategy. Her first run would be about 90 per cent effort to gain a good position in the standings. The second would be all all-out effort.

Rosi pushed off down the mountain on her first run.

She was weaving gracefully around the single flags
and through the gates. To pivot her body quickly and
precisely, she thrust her poles sharply into the ground.
She was "edging" perfectly, placing her skis at an
angle to the snow to hold back speed when coming
into a turn. And when each turn was barely completed,
Rosi swung her momentum toward the next one. She
was racing at about 15 miles per hour, a high speed in
proportion to the constant turns she had to make.

After her first run Rosi was in second place behind her
teammate Pamela Behr. Now Rosi thought she could
win. And in her second run, she breezed through the
hairpin turns and four-gate flushes with cool precision.

A huge crowd lined the slopes, cheering "Rosi, Rosi,
Rosi" as she sped past them down the mountainside.

And when she came to a stop at the bottom, the
winner of the slalom, the crowd went wild with
excitement. Rosi laughed with joy.

Her second run was the fastest of all. Her combined
time had put her well ahead of silver medalist Claudia
Giordani of Italy. Hanni Wenzel of Lichtenstein took
the bronze medal.

After the race, a reporter asked Rosi how she had
done it. "With one gold medal in the pocket," she
laughed, "things go even easier."

Someone else asked if she thought she was winning because of improved technical ability.

"I'd say no," Rosi replied, "but now I have concentration and I'm more relaxed. I love ski racing and since I'm doing what I enjoy, I no longer worry about not doing well."

There were other explanations for Rosi's success. "She is fantastic in her ability to adjust," Claudia Giordani remarked. "If she makes a mistake by leaning too far in one direction and is in danger of missing a gate, she has the strength and technique to correct herself instantly."

Klaus Mayr added: "For many years Rosi would have a great run on part of a course, only to make a mistake that cost split seconds or made her spill. Too often she worried about what times her opponents had made and the possible problems that lay ahead. Today she knows there will be problems and is prepared for them."

Now almost everyone wanted to see Rosi win the giant slalom and become the first woman ever to score a grand-slam in Alpine skiing. Even the parents of little-known Canadian skier Kathy Kreiner were quoted as saying, "Wouldn't it be a shame if somebody prevented Rosi from taking a triple?"

The other skiers, of course, wanted to do just that. They certainly hadn't come all this way to lose. But Rosi was their second choice as gold medalist in the giant slalom.

"If I can't win it," said one of Rosi's rivals, "I hope Granny does. Most of the other girls feel the same way."

By now, the experts predicted Rosi would win. She had the psychological edge on all her opponents so important in skiing—she had mastered the mountain while they had not.

As in the slalom, no practice runs were permitted for the giant slalom. The flags and gates were set, and there were fewer of them than in the slalom. But they were placed along the natural contour of the mountain rather than in the middle of the slope.

The race was about to begin. There was only one run, one chance for Rosi to do it right.

Now it was her turn to go. Rosi passed through gate after gate with lovely, sweeping turns. Her skis were almost never parallel to the ground, but on the extreme edge so as to criss-cross the slope at the highest possible speed. She swept along at 30 miles per hour.

At the middle of the course, Rosi had an amazingly

HOOD COUNTY PUBLIC LIBRARY

fast time of 58.41 seconds. And she looked like the winner. But as she neared the bottom, Rosi came into a gate a bit too sharply. The slight mistake cost her a split-second—and the gold medal. Ironically, it was Kathy Kreiner who beat Rosi by a mere 12/100 of a second. The 18-year-old Canadian had won only one other major race in her life.

Rosi had missed the triple—but that didn't seem to bother her. Smiling, she said, "I'm very happy with the silver. I had not counted on such success." Then Rosi rushed to hug her mother and cried, "When will I believe it, Mother? When?"

After her victory in the slalom, Rosi had been mobbed by her adoring fans. Then she had needed the help of 20 Austrian policemen to get her through the excited crowd.

Now the crush was even worse. The joyous crowd surged around Rosi, eager to be near.

A few days later, the Olympics came to an end. A sleek black limousine had been sent to carry Rosi home.

But Rosi wasn't quite ready to leave Innsbruck. She paused for one last, long look at the mountains surrounding the old city. Her eyes quickly focused on Axamer Lizum, her favorite mountain of them all. She still couldn't believe all that had happened on its steep, icy slopes.

Then it was time to go. As she stepped into the waiting car, Rosi waved to the crowd which had come to say goodbye.

The limousine headed north and soon crossed the Austrian border into West Germany. Sixty miles ahead lay Munich, capital of the province of Bavaria. From there it was only 50 miles to Reit im Winkl.

As the car reached Munich, it slowed nearly to a halt. Thousands of people were milling about the streets of the city, waiting to see Rosi as she passed by. As the limousine inched along, Rosi flashed the dimpled smile made famous in Innsbruck.

At last the limousine left Munich and headed south along the four-lane superhighway called the *Autobahn.* As there was no speed limit, it took less than half an hour before the car turned off to the road which stretched 13 miles to Reit im Winkl.

Over 25,000 cheering people lined the route. And at times Rosi's police escort had difficulty keeping the way clear.

Just before reaching the village, the limousine stopped and Rosi stepped into a horse-drawn carriage covered

with roses. As she entered Reit im Winkl, Rosi was
greeted by another 25,000 well-wishers overrunning
the village square. Among this mass of people, were
the 2,400 inhabitants of Reit im Winkl.

The celebration had begun. The village cannon roared
and the brass band played. A procession of children
came carrying torches.

The local chorus sang ''The Village Has Gone Crazy
with Joy.'' The crowed chanted, ''Golden Rosi, golden
Rosi, do it again.'' The bells of the town rang and rang.

And as it grew dark, Rosi's name was spelled out in
flaming letters on the mountainside.

There was great feasting at the banquet that evening.
Rosi was overwhelmed by it all. And at the dance later
that night she said, ''My God, what would have
happened if I'd won all three gold medals?''

At last it was time for Rosi to go up the mountain to
Winklmoosalm. She looked forward to a few weeks'
rest.

But before long, curiosity seekers from outside arrived
in Reit im Winkl and Winklmoosalm. They pestered
Rosi constantly, knocking at all hours on her door and
peeking through the windows. They became such a
nuisance that soon Rosi was under heavy police
protection.

And she hired a lawyer when she learned that some people were selling unauthorized pictures and posters of her.

Rosi was furious. ''The business rush apparently started when I autographed pictures after competition,'' she told reporters. ''People apparently made mass prints of the material and put it up for sale.'' Reporters from all over were swarming around Rosi, eager to get her story.

Rosi's hopes of seclusion soon vanished, and she decided to leave her home. She had planned to stay longer before going to the United States to continue racing on the World Cup tour. But it just couldn't be.

Before Rosi left for America, a costume ball was given in her honor in Munich. She selected her costume carefully; she came as a harem girl with a veil to hide her famous face. But reporters and fans recognized her anyway.

''Oh my,'' she said. ''I do hope the pressure will die down now that I am off to the U.S.''

Rosi first went to Lake Tahoe, on the California-Nevada border, hoping for a quiet vacation from the demanding crowds. But there was just as much excitement at Lake Tahoe as there had been everywhere else. She was given standing ovations when she came down to the hotel dining room.

Rosi continued on to Copper Mountain, Colorado, the twelfth of fourteen stops on the World Cup tour. All along, she had said that her aim in 1976 was to win the overall World Cup title. As much as she prized her Olympic victories, Rosi felt that they didn't prove as much about her ability.

Rosi was still surrounded by throngs of reporters and grasping fans. But if she was feeling the pressure, she didn't show it.

She won both the giant slalom and the slalom. With these two victories, Rosi had captured the overall championship and the slalom title. And she had moved into second place in the giant slalom standings. In her honor, the course was renamed "Rosi's Run."

After the World Cup finally ended in March, Rosi returned to Munich. There she was asked if she would now give up amateur skiing.

"I've got to think over things thoroughly," she replied after a moment. "Ski racing is great fun and I still do like it. Maybe in the summer I will get the itch to start training. I just don't know."

Then Rosi went home again. The ski season was over and the tourists had gone. Perhaps she could find solitude there once again. Perhaps there would be moonlit nights when the only sound to be heard was the song of the wind.

CREATIVE EDUCATION SPORTS SUPERSTARS

Superstars! Superstars! Superstars!

Football
Johnny Unitas
Bob Griese
Vince Lombardi
Joe Namath
O. J. Simpson
Fran Tarkenton
Roger Staubach
Alan Page
Larry Csonka
Don Shula
Franco Harris
Terry Bradshaw
Chuck Foreman

Baseball
Frank Robinson
Tom Seaver
Jackie Robinson
Johnny Bench
Hank Aaron
Roberto Clemente
Mickey Mantle
Rod Carew
Fred Lynn
Pete Rose

Basketball
Walt Frazier
Kareem Abdul Jabbar
Wilt Chamberlain
Jerry West
Bill Russell
Bill Walton
Bob McAdoo
Julius Erving
John Havlicek
Rick Barry
George McGinnis

Tennis
Jimmy Connors
Chris Evert
Pancho Gonzales
Evonne Goolagong
Arthur Ashe
Billie Jean King
Stan Smith

Racing
Peter Revson
Jackie Stewart
A. J. Foyt
Richard Petty

Miscellaneous
Mark Spitz
Muhammad Ali
Secretariat
Olga Korbut
Evel Knievel
Jean Claude Killy
Janet Lynn
Peggy Fleming
Pelé
Rosi Mittermaier
Sheila Young
Dorothy Hamill
Nadia Comaneci

Golf
Lee Trevino
Jack Nicklaus
Arnold Palmer
Johnny Miller
Kathy Whitworth
Laura Baugh

Hockey
Phil and Tony Esposito
Gordie Howe
Bobby Hull
Bobby Orr